GRADE

1

The Syllabus of Examinations should be read for details of requirements, especially those for scales, aural tests and sight-reading. Attention should be paid to the Special Notices on the inside front cover, where warning is given of any changes.

The syllabus is obtainable from music retailers or from The Associated Board of the Royal Schools of Music, 24 Portland Place, London W1B 1LU (please send a stamped addressed C5 (162mm × 229mm) envelope).

In examination centres outside the UK, information and syllabuses may be obtained from the Local Representative.

CONTENTS

Where appropriate, pieces in this volume have been checked with original source material and edited as necessary for instructional purposes. Fingering, phrasing, bowing, metronome marks and the editorial realization of ornaments (where given) are for guidance but are not comprehensive or obligatory.

DO NOT
PHOTOCOPY
© MUSIC

Alternative pieces for this grade

Music origination by Jack Thompson.
Cover by Økvik Design.
Printed in England by Halstan & Co. Ltd, Amersham, Bucks.

 A:1

Go from my window

Arranged by
Edward Huws Jones

ANON. ENGLISH

15·01·01

This melody was immensely popular with Elizabethan and Jacobean composers and was arranged for lute, keyboard, viols and other instruments. The accompaniment in this arrangement draws on settings attributed to Thomas Morley and John Munday in the *Fitzwilliam Virginal Book.* EHJ

Noel Nouvelet

A:2

Arranged by
Edward Huws Jones

ANON. FRENCH

Noel Nouvelet (which can be translated as 'Christmas comes again') is a French carol from the 15th century. The melody has a dignified, processional quality, and suggests an accompaniment of drones – such as might be played by bagpipes or a hurdy-gurdy. EHJ

A:3

A Little Dance

from Act 1 of *The Unexpected Meeting*

Arranged by
Watson Forbes

GLUCK

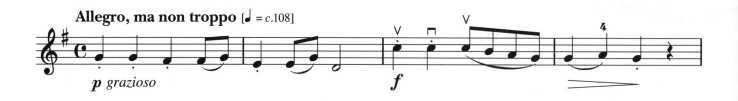

This attractive dance comes from Gluck's French comic opera *La Rencontre Imprévue (The Unexpected Meeting)*, which was first performed in Vienna in 1764.

Reproduced from *A First Book of Classical and Romantic Pieces* by permission. All enquiries for this piece apart from the examinations should be addressed to Oxford University Press, Music Department, Great Clarendon Street, Oxford, OX2 6DP.

Song Without Words

No. 8 from *First String Tunes*

B:1

CARSE

Adam Carse, a professor of harmony and counterpoint at the Royal Academy of Music, 1922–40, is perhaps best-known for his study of the history of instruments and the orchestra. In 1947 he donated his collection of around 350 historic wind instruments to the Horniman Museum, London.

© 1914 by Stainer & Bell Ltd
Reproduced by permission. All enquiries for this piece apart from the examinations should be addressed to Stainer & Bell Ltd, PO Box 110, Victoria House, 23 Gruneisen Road, London N3 1DZ.

A Keltic Song

No. 20 from *20 Tunes for Beginners*

PALMER
and BEST

Morningtown Ride

B:3

Arranged by Peter Davey
and Timothy Roberts

REYNOLDS

Morningtown Ride is a song by the American folk singer and songwriter Malvina Reynolds. It tells the story of a train that takes sleeping children safely through the night to Morningtown.

Reproduced by kind permission of Amadeo-Brio Music Inc., administered by Leosong Copyright Service Ltd. All enquiries for this piece apart from the examinations should be addressed to Leosong Copyright Service Ltd. 5th Floor, 13 Berners Street, London W1T 3LH.

8

C:1

Sharks

EDWARD HUWS JONES

Sharks is an assertive piece and calls for a lot of bow, even on the quavers. In the middle section the player needs to save bow at the *start* of the dotted minim, in order to create a spectacular crescendo! EHJ

© 1996 by Faber Music Ltd

Reproduced from *Going Solo – Violin* by permission. All enquiries for this piece apart from the examinations should be addressed to Faber Music Ltd, 3 Queen Square, London WC1N 3AU.

Lullaby

No. 2 from *24 Easy Little Concert Pieces*

SZELÉNYI

Clog Dance

No. 3 from *More Travel Tunes*

MARGERY DAWE

This tune is quite heavy in character – remember the dancers are wearing clogs rather than ballet shoes! There are good opportunities for different bowing effects, especially the lifted up bows in the first two bars.

Checklist of Scales and Arpeggios

Candidates and teachers may find this checklist useful in learning the requirements of the grade. Full details of the forms of the various requirements, including details of rhythms, starting notes and bowing patterns, are given in the syllabus and in the scale books published by the Board.

Grade 1

			separate bows						slurred					
									two quavers to a bow					
Major Scales	**D Major**	1 Octave												
	A Major	1 Octave												
	G Major	2 Octaves												
									not applicable					
Major Arpeggios	**D Major**	1 Octave												
	A Major	1 Octave												
	G Major	2 Octaves												

Printed by
Halstan & Co. Ltd., Amersham, Bucks.